Unless otherwise noted, Scripture is take from the ESV Bible (The Holy Bible, English Standard Version), copyright 2001by Crossway, a publishing ministry of Good News Publishers. Used by permission. All rights reserved.

Book design by Tobi Carter
Photographs courtesy of Angela Fountain

ISBN 978-1-7361608-0-0 (paperback)
ISBN 978-1-7361608-2-4 (hardcover)
ISBN 978-1-7361608-1-7 (e-book)
ISBN 978-1-7361608-3-1 (audio)

Daughter, You Are...

10-Day Devotional for Women
Words of Encouragement and Inspiration
(You Are Not What They Say You Are)

By Sherri Thorpe

May the Lord
be your strength!
Love in Christ!
Sherri

Dedication

Dr. Earlie E. Thorpe — For your love of history, the Word of God, and giving me the inspiration to write at an early age. I thank God I had the opportunity of having your presence in my life.

Aunt Martha Vivian Thorpe — Thank you for being one of my biggest supporters, encouraging me to write, and loving me so much. I love you so very much too!

The Beautiful Women of Memorial Presbyterian Church, Roosevelt, New York — Thank you for the beauty of you. You do not understand how so many of you have carried me through hard times and struggles with a hug, a smile, and encouraging words.

Chantal Jones — To someone who was a wonderful and dear friend. You were such a blessing in my life. You are now another angel in Heaven above.

Contents

A Letter to You

"And he said unto her, Daughter, be of good comfort:
thy faith hath made thee whole; go in peace."
— *Luke 8:48, King James Bible*

Dear Sister,

I call you my sister as each of us is a strong, amazing and powerful sister to every woman we share this world with. Together we are united and form an intricate link from one to one another, through our hearts and spirit.

It is my sincere pleasure to share these writings with you. For quite a while, the Lord has been speaking to my heart to write this book. I write it from the love of Christ flowing through my heart to yours. My purpose is to share how special we are in the eyes and heart of our Creator.

As we live our lives, we encounter so many challenges through words, images, and experiences. We are inundated with what a woman should look like, sound like, dress like, and even feel like. We hear this information from our friends, family, coworkers, and the media. In the sea of all we are told, we sometimes receive in our hearts these ideas of what others think we ought to be. We may have moments where comments made to us by someone causes us to stop and look at ourselves twice in a mirror, questioning who we are. Other times, there are words said that are so hurtful we dislike what we once liked about ourselves. We are bombarded by magazine articles, television programs on beauty, commercials telling us that, if we do not use this or that product, we will become less than what they think we should be. Also, the entertainment industry is constantly influencing the latest styles and one's mindset toward relationships - so much so that who knows what to do or think?

There are days when we wonder what we should be to ourselves besides just someone's mother, daughter, wife, sister, grandmother, friend or coworker. Sometimes it seems like, no matter what, there is no rest and we feel what we are doing is just not enough. When we are at that place emotionally and someone says words that strike a chord of doubt in our hearts, we can become angry, spiteful, and some-what bitter. Other times we carry it to the point we begin to become fearful and depressed.

In the scripture above, Jesus is speaking to a woman who has suffered from bleeding for twelve long years. She was menstruating and this issue would not stop. The requirement during that time period was for a woman to touch no one. They con-sidered her unclean. Normally, after seven days, by which time in which her menstruation should be over, she could resume her place in society and her daily activities. Yet, this was not the case for this woman. In those twelve long years, she lived isolated from others as her ongoing bleeding meant that no one was allowed to touch her. Doctors could not help her, for those she went to made her problem worse, and the sorrow and depression from her situation was difficult to endure.

When Jesus said "Daughter" to this woman, he re-ferred to her with a word that meant, in those times, to be endearing and full of love. The woman, through her faith in Jesus and her desire for acceptance and to feel loved again, mattered.

We all desire love, encouragement, to hear a kind word, and to be understood and cared about. There are places in our hearts that long for healing. When the woman with the issue of blood was healed and heard the word "Daughter" from Jesus, the Son of God, He also restored her mentally, emotionally and spiritually. How? Imagine not hearing even for one day, year after year, a kind word or the opportunity for human contact. Her faith in Jesus restored her physical being, and His gentle words healed her emotional pain.

In the following chapters, the Lord led me to write these words to help heal those parts of your heart needing restoration. May they resonate in your mind and encourage you as often as they have done for me as I wrote them.

Blessings to you always,
Sherri

Foreword

Your issue is not your identity! Those words sum up the message of this powerful devotional book, aimed at helping women created in the image of God to reclaim their rightful identity as "daughter." Issues are something that no person can completely avoid. The word "issue" is used to describe a burden or a problem someone carries, with the implication that this person rarely has the strength to deal with it on their own. Issues can rob us of the abundant life, destiny, and potential that God has prepared us for. Issues are obstacles that don't allow us to produce and develop for the purpose we're destined to be in life.

Moreover, the enemy of our soul loves to use our issues to mar the image of who God has created us to be. As Ms. Thorpe points out, the woman at the center of the story in Luke 8 lived in a situation other people had determined her worth based on their definition of her dysfunction. They viewed her as a religious and social outcast who did not have the right to decide her own worth. It forced her to cooperate with rules set up based on society's perception of her problem. We don't even know her name. All we know is that she was a woman who had issues.

If you are reading this book, your current situation or issue may look like it has defined you. If you have allowed other people to define you based on what they know about you, if you've let other people determine your destiny based on what they think of you, if your issues have you feeling isolated like an outcast or if you find other's definition of your issues to become your definition over your life, prepare to change.

Every word written is a challenge to the reader to see themselves the way God sees them--through the lens of Jesus Christ. You are so much more than who "you" say you are. This book is not just a message of encouragement that the author has written, but it's the calling unto which a woman lives for - it is about Christian hope and encouragement brought into the lives of God's women. As her pastor, I've witnessed it firsthand.

Daughter, may the words of these pages bless you, and may you rise above every label placed upon you and break every chain that attempts to hold you down.

Rev. Dr. Patrick Daymond
Pastor, Covenant United Church of Christ

Daughter, You Are...

Unbreakable

*"It is because of the LORD'S loving kindnesses that
we are not consumed, Because His [tender] compassions
never fail." — Lamentations 3:22, Amplified Bible*

Dear Daughter,

There are things that come at us, and we wonder why. It could be something our parents, a friend, a co-worker, spouse, or even what the driver in the next car at the stoplight did to set the start of our day from peaceful to painful, where we are in a helpless heap, ready to cry, if not already crying. You are now in the mode of trying to figure out what happened, why was it said, and how to internally repair your heart so you do not hold on to the very incident or words that brought you to the place you are now. No one wants to feel consumed and think all day and night about the grief someone else placed on their heart.

Jesus, speaking to my heart, said this:

"*The woman that was partially kneeling towards me to touch the hem of my robe--I did not see her but I felt her. I felt more than just her faith. I felt the words she longed to hear during her twelve-year bout with her physical sickness. Her sorrow was like an ocean that could not reach the seashore to bring her rest. For twelve long years, she took people telling her she was nothing while she endured her external pain. No one reached out to touch her. No one tried to hold her close and--although this was part of her society's tradition because of her physical state-- it hurt her. It hurt her because she had no control over her problem. She did not know why it happened, and over time resented it. She knew she did nothing to cause her situation, and she no longer desired the uncaring treatment because of it.*

Maybe someone has said or done something to hurt you. Well, my daughter, you are not alone. I am with you. I want you to take several deep breaths and let it go. I am here with you, and I heard and saw what they did. So, today and always, I ask you to come closer to me and let me put my arms around you. One way I am here to do this is when you come to me in prayer. The other way is my words. Do not allow ugly words to consume you. Trust in me with all your heart. Do not embrace the words or actions that came into your moments of living. Let it go and recover quickly."

As I received these words from Jesus, I want you to know, today, you are whole. Let your heart be strong in the Lord and he will give you strength. You are resilient. Your help comes from and is great in him because he lives in your heart. Do not get angry but hold on to his loving kindness. As you hold on to him, he is holding onto you and, in this, you will not fall. Today, in Jesus, you are unbreakable.

Reflection:

Think about and write down how you see yourself as strong and *Unbreakable*.

_____

_____

_____

_____

_____

_____

_____

_____

_____

_____

_____

_____

_____

_____

_____

_____

_____

_____

_____

Daughter, You Are...

Beautiful

"I will praise thee; for I am fearfully and wonderfully made: marvelous are thy works; and that my soul knoweth right well." — Psalm 139:14, King James Bible

"But the LORD said to Samuel, "Do not look at his appearance or at the height of his stature, because I have rejected him. For the LORD sees not as man sees; for man looks at the outward appearance, but the LORD looks at the heart." — 1 Samuel 16:7, Amplified Bible

Dear Daughter,

Jesus, speaking to my heart, said this:

"You are beautiful. You are fearfully and wonderfully made in the image of my Father. You are not a mistake. I see the wonderful things I created you to do and be. You have a purpose. Where you are in your life

does not define you. You are on a journey. I design all journeys to lead you to me. They are paths that allow me to touch your heart. Sometimes the road is difficult, but trust in me with all your heart."

I know you work hard to look perfect on the outside. There are so many different kinds of make-up, clothing, perfumes, and hairstyles to wear. Yet, I see how you are trying to cover up, through these things, the hurt in your heart. Sometimes we feel that what we do on the outside will make up for what we want to feel on the inside. It seems fine to look good on the outside, and for a while we feel better. Then something or someone comes along doing or saying something to remind us of our internal hurt. There are many fiery darts that come at different times and in distinct ways to bring us down."

My child, come closer to me and draw your heart near mine. Let me release the pain so you can live with joy and peace. I will teach you how you mean so much. As you reach for my Word, I will write my promises upon your heart. I will build up the inner you and transform your heart to praise and see how you are a masterpiece. I will not let someone take your joy. I will hold tightly onto your hand and keep your head up."

Beauty is in the eye of the beholder. I behold all the beauty you are as you were created first in the flow of my Father's heart. This is the time your heartbeat *truly existed. Where you are positioned on earth is the place, I desire you to be. It is not to destroy you, but to give you hope and understanding."*

God loves and understands who each of us are. How his words are so affirming to me and I hope they touched your heart as well. Our beauty is beyond our eyes, hair and what we wear. We are beautiful spirits connected to God. He really loves us so much and we do not have to prove our beauty as we are simply beautiful not just at this moment but always.

Reflection:

As God sees our beauty, how do you see how wonderful and *Beautiful* you are?

_____

_____

_____

_____

_____

_____

_____

_____

_____

_____

_____

_____

_____

_____

_____

_____

_____

_____

_____

Daughter, You Are...

Worthy

"See what an incredible quality of love the Father has shown to us, that we would [be permitted to] be named and called and counted the children of God! And so, we are! For this reason, the world does not know us, because it did not know Him." — 1 John 3:1, Amplified Bible

Dear Daughter,

Words can cut through someone's heart like a knife. So, they say you are not good enough? They say you need to be better? Oh, how the pain of someone's words and actions wound our minds and spirit. It is like they bring a negative spirit to steal your happiness. You may stop awhile and go to a quiet corner to assess the damage. In that time of review, we find we may take our own assessment, add a few extra touches of past hurts and bits of bitterness, drawing an even bigger picture than the one just given by someone else's ugliness. After all, someone saying you do not matter as much as you think hurts. The wave of hurt brings up questions on whether what they said or did is true. Was there any truth spoken in the heat of the moment? The answer is "no." The complete answer from God is absolutely "no."

Jesus, speaking to my heart, said this:

"The day you are born you are worthy. You are worthy to be kissed, hugged, fed, read to, washed, pampered, and put safely to bed for a restful sleep, where you wake up again to another day, another tomorrow. Each day we live in—that day has value. In all of your daily living I have given you life because you are worthy. You exist because I fell in love with the thought of you. You are mine and my love for you does not exist in the realms of what this world sees you as. You exist in my eyes and heart as an amazing life giving life to those around you. You are to live in the understanding of me and not what people try to measure you to be."

People can look at one another, but, as the saying goes, no one can tell a book by its cover. When we have Christ as our Savior, it covers us under a beautiful light. It is the light of his love that guides us, helps us, heals us, and lets us know we are a unique creation. Through him, all things are possible and made new. There is nothing that can separate us from his love. He is the forgiveness we need when others will not forgive us, and the times of understanding when we find it hard to forgive ourselves. The love that God gives says we are worthy to begin again, to reject the meanness of others, and to let go of self-hatred.

God knows we want so much to understand and be understood. We want to understand why people would want to put someone else down, hurt others, and take away someone's happiness. Let us understand many times it is not about us, but about the hurts in the hearts of other people. The other person may be going through their own litany of questions and not seeing their own worth. Well, in Christ we are worthy and, as long as we have him in our lives, we are strong and we matter. You are worthy, so live in God's love and do not hold on to the things from this world that hurt you.

Let go and let God's words define your purpose and manner of existing. Others did not place you here—God did. Seek his love and trust, knowing you will be found. See, in God you were never lost because all the time he was waiting for you just to tell you: "Daughter, you are worthy."

Reflection:

You are precious to God, so how do you see how important and *Worthy* you are?

_____

_____

_____

_____

_____

_____

_____

_____

_____

_____

_____

_____

_____

_____

_____

_____

_____

_____

_____

_____

_____

Daughter, You Are...
Undefeated

"But his delight is in the law of the Lord, And on His law [His precepts and teachings] he [habitually] meditates day and night. And he will be like a tree firmly planted [and fed] by streams of water, which yields its fruit in its season; Its leaf does not wither; And in whatever he does, he prospers [and comes to maturity]." — Psalm 1:2-3, Amplified Bible

Dear Daughter,

Jesus, speaking to my heart, said this:

"I do not design challenges that come to harm you, but to carry you through to the place I need you to be. During this journey, hold on to my words. I care about your battles and how hard they can be but, no matter what, you are undefeated. You are this powerful spirit because my Spirit dwells within you. Let my words be your fists instead of your anger being your guide. Let

my words break down doors and crush words that people have placed in your way to cause you to trip and fall.

In me you are a warrior—strong, bright and invincible. My Son came into this world to save it. So, you are saved from the pain that others attempt to cause. You are saved from the worries and fears others try to instill in your heart and mind, causing you to second-guess yourself. In me, you are like a tree with strong roots, for in me you are immovable. As long as you hold on to me, the path you are on will be made perfect with my love leading the way. I have your best interest at heart and nothing can change this.

Daughter, there was a woman named Esther. I wrote her story to tell how she was a woman who used wisdom and stayed dedicated in her life to Me. She loved who she was and who she represented, even though she was in a foreign land. She used her position to make sure others would not come to any harm. Her love and trust for me never changed, regardless of the circumstances. See, it is not the issues we face that are the problem; it is how we act and react to them that can cause us stress, disappointment, unrest, and defeat. Let every challenge position you to stand tall and take what comes. Esther was a symbol of bravery for many and she is this for you today, too.

Today, be a sturdy rock and let nothing cause you to stumble. I know times can be hard, get hard, and *try to knock the wind out of your sail of success. Well, I call out to you, daughter, to stand on my wisdom. Daily pray, praise, and love me. I am with you and love you very much. When others try to steal your victory through words and cruel actions, just smile and keep moving. Do not let their ways towards you define your success. Look only to me and there you will find your undefeated victory. For through your trust and hope in me you will always be undefeated."*

Reflection:

During days of difficulty, how do you overcome and are *Undefeated?*

_____

_____

_____

_____

_____

_____

_____

_____

_____

_____

_____

_____

_____

_____

_____

_____

_____

_____

_____

_____

Daughter, You Are...
Miraculous

"But let it be [the inner beauty of] the hidden person of the heart, with the imperishable quality and unfading charm of a gentle and peaceful spirit, [one that is calm and self-controlled, not overanxious, but serene and spiritually mature] which is very precious in the sight of God." — 1 Peter 3:4, Amplified Bible

Dear Daughter,

Jesus, speaking to my heart, said this:

"You are a miracle. When I thought of you, I knew you would be a special gift. You are a rare individual of unique ability. I give you my words, written in love, to learn and discover all of who you are in Me, yourself, and this world. You came into this world just as you should be. There are no errors. I know this world tells you what you need to change to measure up, ac-

cording to its standards. Do not get caught up in those whispers. They are not the truths you need to hear and believe.

Each day comes and the dawning of it is new. It is new for you to experience, embrace, and say to it, 'This is the day that the Lord has made. I will rejoice in it. I will make it what it needs to be in the eyes of the Lord that loves me.' Yes, daughter, I love you. I love you in the struggles you have and what you work at aspiring to be. I will tell you I love you as often as I can. My love protects you. My love brings you peace. My love is for you to tell you to continue in this race of living. Continue to mold your heart to the love of my words. The more you do this, the more precious you become.

Miracles are miracles to show others they can happen. When you were born, you were a special event. Your entrance into this world was chosen and was precisely at the time you needed to be here. Your life radiates with many possibilities. Your life force matters, and it is here to influence the lives of others around you. Your living is a testament that I am real. There are miracles inside of you waiting to be birthed from your heart into the life you are living. My spirit inside you longs to live and push through to bless you. Miracles happen when someone believes and allows them to occur."

We see in life how it is possible for miracles to happen and when they do, they are not forgotten. They are remembered and leave an indelible impression on our soul. Miracles have happened in my life and as they happen in yours, we see how the miracle of God's love leaves an imprint on our words, thoughts, hopes, dreams, understanding, and beliefs. God, the author of miracles teaches us and how he is here for us ready to make the impossible possible.

We are God's daughters, made in his love – so we are not a mistake. We are a miracle crafted out of the miracle of God's love and grace. Let us think on our miraculous existence when someone holds us in their arms tightly. It reminds us how Jesus loves and what he sees us as - a lovely daughter to hold close to his heart. Each of us are the miracle of his heart.

Reflection:

Think about moments where you see how important and *Miraculous* your life is.

_____

_____

_____

_____

_____

_____

_____

_____

_____

_____

_____

_____

_____

_____

_____

_____

_____

_____

Daughter, You Are...

"But seek ye first the kingdom of God, and his righteousness; and all these things shall be added unto you." — Matthew 6:33, King James Bible

"Delight thyself also in the Lord: and he shall give thee the desires of thine heart." — Psalm 37:4, King James Bible

Dear Daughter,

Jesus, speaking to my heart, said this:

"Work hard each day following my precepts in saving money: to not be a borrower so as to avoid being a slave to the lenders of this world; give unselfishly to others; and give the first fruits of your earnings to your church home so they can continue the ministries built up in the Gospel of Jesus Christ. The wealth

you gain I will give and, as you trust me, you will see how I stand by my Word. In all you do, you need to do it cheerfully, without complaint. When something is needed, pray and I will answer. The foundation of all wealth is trust. Trust in my promises, trust in my answers, and trust in my wisdom. Do not worry how I will answer—only that you know through me it has already been answered.

Daughter, develop your wealth in my Spirit and I will add all things desired into your life.

The world has much to say about wealth and the superficial glory that comes from owning material things. The world says the more one has, the more successful they are. The world says that, only one who owns this or that name brand is worthy of being considered the best. Well, this is not true. Wealth is not found in the accumulation of money and the things it can buy or the people it can change. Wealth is the home in your heart where my love dwells. The issues of life flow from the heart. So, will your abundance rest in kindness, forgiveness, understanding, hope, joy, peace, generosity, and love in your heart? Wealth is more about how your heart matures in the spirit of my love."

Let not your happiness rely on feelings. Feelings can be deceptive and money can bring temporary pleasures, but also a lifetime of woes. What we are all called to do is learn how to live for and towards one another. Wealth is not solely for the pursuance of self. Wealth of any kind is meant to be shared and, the more one gives, the more one receives in return.

The art of pursuing is important. It is the daily lesson of learning what is the most important thing to give to others and ourselves in words and actions. Jesus is the answer, and you are the vessel carrying his answers to the world. Intellect is the home of knowledge, but the truth of knowledge is how it is used. God gives his Word in love to show us how to use his wisdom in this world, as he is the author of it and our intelligence. God has given each member of humanity this gift, but it is in the manner of how they use and apply it.

Today, let us count the blessings of smiles, kisses and hugs received knowing God has already provided for our needs.

Reflection:

How are you a rare jewel and *Wealthy* in love and hope?

_____

_____

_____

_____

_____

_____

_____

_____

_____

_____

_____

_____

_____

_____

_____

_____

_____

_____

_____

Daughter, You Are...

Promised

"And we know [with great confidence] that God
[who is deeply concerned about us] causes all things
to work together [as a plan] for good for those who
love God, to those who are called according to His plan
and purpose." — Romans 8:28, Amplified Bible

"Blessed [gratefully praised and adored] be the God
and Father of our Lord Jesus Christ, the Father of
mercies and the God of all comfort, 4 who comforts and
encourages us in every trouble so that we will be able
to comfort and encourage those who are in any kind of
trouble, with the comfort with which we ourselves are
comforted by God." — 2 Corinthians 1:3-4, Amplified Bible

Dear Daughter,
    Jesus, speaking to my heart, said this:
    "You are here not just to be here but to be loved,
and you are promised. I already promised in my heart

before you were created in my love to be cared for, watched over, and blessed. In the Salvation of my Son I made you special in my heart and to receive every promise spoken in my Word. I do not break my promises; I keep them and carry them out.

I have promised it to wake you to see the dawning of each day.

I have promised it to give you life and life more abundantly in my Grace and Mercy.

I have promised it to heal you when you are sick.

I have promised it to order your footsteps as you come closer in relationship with me."

I have promised it to allow no harm to come to you.

I have promised it that my care for you is greater than the birds of the air and the lilies in the field.

I have promised that I will give provision supplying all of your needs.

I have promised that I will always give you rest and calm all your fears.

I have promised it I can transform your life.

I have promised I can increase your territory.

I have promised I will always love you.

You are a promised child of mine, so let your heart rest in all the promises of my Word. I never promised easy. I promised wisdom, help, understanding, guidance, and comfort. Each day when you rise, and before you rest your head to sleep, seek, study, and recite these promises in your heart, mind, and tongue."

Let us speak the promises of the Lord over our life; see what power they have and how they can change the issues in our life. See, for our life is not an ordinary one, but a promised one filled with endless blessings. May we never be discouraged as we rest in and allow the promises of God to encourage us.

Reflection:

Where do you see the desire of leading a life as a *Promised* child of God?

_____

_____

_____

_____

_____

_____

_____

_____

_____

_____

_____

_____

_____

_____

_____

_____

_____

_____

_____

_____

_____

_____

_____

_____

_____

_____

_____

_____

_____

_____

_____

_____

_____

_____

_____

_____

_____

_____

_____

_____

_____

_____

_____

_____

Daughter, You Are...
Healed

"The Spirit of the Lord is upon me, because he hath anointed me to preach the gospel to the poor; he hath sent me to heal the brokenhearted, to preach deliverance to the captives, and recovering of sight to the blind, to set at liberty them that are bruised." — Luke 4:18, King James Bible

Dear Daughter,

Let us proclaim: "We are healed!" We can carry many scars, but they are not just external. The scars we carry are also within: they are within our minds and words, and reflect in our actions. When the woman with the issue of blood came to Jesus and touched the hem of his garment, Jesus looked down. He looked down because he felt in his heart that the woman who touched him, did so with determination because she was desperate for help. Jesus sensed her feelings of inadequacy and loneliness, as well as the brokenness in her spirit. Jesus looked down so his gaze could meet hers. He needed to look into her eyes so she could see the love in his. Jesus looked down so she would look up, away from her circumstances.

Jesus, speaking to my heart, said this:

"Who hurt you today? Who lied to you today? Who looked at you and searched for words to tear down your heart? The hurting words they found were from the reservoir of pain they have been carrying from their past hurts. I can see beyond their hearts the clandestine place they have held onto their pain. They have been feeding off of it and it has dictated their relationships. Daughter, do not receive the hurt they are trying to transfer to you. Reach for my written words to protect and do surgery on your mental, emotional, and physical well-being. Through my Spirit, healing begins from the inside out. The woman who touched me had not received any expression of love for twelve long years. Her tranquility, joy, and trust dried up a long time ago, like soil becoming parched without water, before she searched for me."

Daughter, you are healed. I speak to you like I spoke to the woman who touched my garment. Whether your pain in your heart has happened for a moment or many years before, I ask that you please let it go. In me, "no weapon formed against you shall prosper."

Words and action have power, but only based on the amount of power you give them. Will you hold on to anger, bitterness, or ideas of revenge? Who will doing so profit? Forgive and let go, as I was lovingly telling the woman who came to, me. I did not want her hurt to be magnified beyond her physical healing. It was important that her physical and spiritual healing was simultaneous."

"Many are the afflictions of the righteous:
but the Lord delivereth him out of them all."
— Psalm 34:19, King James Bible

Let us seek after and come to the Lord. Let us allow his words to heal us so we can continue on, for God wants us to succeed and no one to steal our joy. His Word is our armor of protection to ward off any negative plan or attack against us. In the Lord, whatever was meant for destruction—in our lives he will turn it into joy.

Today, we know we are healed. Nothing and no one can take it away. Through God, we are restored.

Reflection:

What words and things do you allow to restore you and be *Healed* in your heart?

_____

_____

_____

_____

_____

_____

_____

_____

_____

_____

_____

_____

_____

_____

_____

_____

_____

_____

_____

_____

Daughter, You Are...

Forgiven

*"For You, O Lord, are good, and ready to forgive
[our sins, sending them away, completely letting them
go forever and ever]; And abundant in lovingkindness
and overflowing in mercy to all those who call
upon You." — Psalm 86:5, Amplified Bible*

*"Even if he sins against you seven times a day, and returns
to you seven times and says, 'I repent,' you must forgive
him [that is, give up resentment and consider the offense
recalled and annulled]." — Luke 17:4, Amplified Bible*

Dear Daughter,

Jesus, speaking to my heart, said this:

*"The woman who came to me who was physical-
ly bent down low and my endearing words healed her
spirit—I was also telling her to forgive. She needed to*

forgive those that said spiteful things due to her condition. She took those words, which isolated her heart, deeply. She remembered all the times of exclusion and being forgotten. As long as people knew of her physical state, they had no intentions of easing her circumstances by one word or act of kindness. She understood that she was not going to be included until her physical plight changed, but she hoped and prayed. She wanted someone to understand and take just a moment to care.

Regardless of all the things that have happened with others, do not hold a grudge. There are times we may feel someone owes us an apology: someone said something against you; someone did not do as they said they would; someone lied; someone cheated; or someone stole. Come to me and let me bring light into the darkness that others brought you."

"You shall not take vengeance or bear a grudge against the sons of your own people, but you shall love your neighbor as yourself "— Leviticus 19:18, English Standard Bible

"If the woman with the issue of blood after being healed internally and externally did not forgive—she would still be sick. By coming to me, she was ready to let go of many things and my word of 'daughter' confirmed this for her. All hurts are threefold. It is the

mental (mind), spiritual (heart), and physical (body) that needs repair. Forgiveness is not letting the sun go down upon your anger. Forgiveness is not looking back. Forgiveness is being forgetful—it is not a reminder to repeat to others, or yourself, what took place repeatedly. Forgiveness is freedom for you. It is to break the chains of hurt that held you down.

The woman with the issue of blood may have been bent over by years of humiliation, but in me she was pulled up to stand straight and strong, and know those times were over."

In Christ, you are forgiven. You are forgiven of regrets, anger, bitterness, and despair. In him there is a life more abundant and beautiful but, if one holds on to the past, they can lose sight of Jesus. Daughter, in Christ, means forgiveness can begin. It allows every day lived to be a fresh one. Let today be the beginning so that in Jesus you are healed.

"Whenever you stand praying, if you have anything against anyone, forgive him [drop the issue, let it go], so that your Father who is in heaven will also forgive you your transgressions and wrongdoings [against Him and others]." — Mark 11:25, Amplified Bible

Reflection:

How can we be honest and have a heart that has *Forgiven* ourselves and others?

_____

_____

_____

_____

_____

_____

_____

_____

_____

_____

_____

_____

_____

_____

_____

_____

_____

_____

_____

Daughter, You Are...

Loved

"For God so loved the world, that he gave his only begotten Son, that whosoever believeth in him should not perish, but have everlasting life." — John 3:16, King James Bible

"An excellent woman [one who is spiritual, capable, intelligent, and virtuous], who is he who can find her? Her value is more precious than jewels and her worth is far above rubies or pearls." — Proverbs 31:10. Amplified Bible

Dear Daughter,

Jesus, speaking to my heart, said this:

"You are my darling daughter, and you are so loved. When you were born in my thoughts, you are loved. Nothing can take this away. I could not wait for you to meet the place I created for you. I have been watching over you ever since you came into this world. I have seen every teardrop, every frown, and every smile.

I have heard every laugh, shout, and whisper. I have seen all your joyful, fearful, and angry moments. My eyes have never stopped watching over you then, and they are watching over you now. I know the pathways in life have not been easy to travel and there will be many more bridges you will need to cross. In these times you have felt I was far from you, but nothing could be further from the truth, for I am always near."

In a person's life there are many falls that will occur. One falls as they first learn to walk, as they learn to ride a bike, or even learn to wear high-heeled shoes. But no matter what type of fall you have; I am here to catch you. In every fall you have, whether a painful or a light sting, my love is waiting to hold you close. My love is there to protect and heal every wound you receive.

I need you to know that, in the landscape of life, there is beauty. There is the beauty of my love even as the world seems to be tumbling down. My love for you is telling you not to give up, to hold my words like you would hold a friend's hand in yours, and to keep believing that, through me, things always get better. Living life in the world does not have the answers, but living life in the world through me provides every answer you need to overcome it. My presence in your life can even help you to overcome the struggles you are having now—at this every moment.

My daughter, my love is abundant and can be applied to anything you are going through. When you apply my Word to everything you are facing, you give me the opportunity to face it with you. Your presence in this world makes a difference through me."

When difficult moments come, please think on these words:

"I look up toward the mountains. Where can I find help? My help comes from the LORD, the maker of heaven and earth. He will not let you fall. Your guardian will not fall asleep. Indeed, the Guardian of Israel never rests or sleeps. The LORD is your guardian. The LORD is the shade over your right hand.   The sun will not beat down on you during the day, nor will the moon at night. The LORD guards you from every evil. He guards your life. The LORD guards you as you come and go, now and forever." — Psalm 121, Good Word Translation Bible

"The Lord is my shepherd; I shall not want. He makes me lie down in green pastures. He leads me beside still waters. He restores my soul. He leads me in paths of righteousness for his name's sake. Even though I walk through the valley of the shadow of death, I will fear no evil, for you are with me; your rod and your staff, they comfort me. You prepare a table before me in the presence of my enemies; you anoint my head with oil; my

cup overflows. *Surely goodness and mercy shall follow me all the days of my life, and I shall dwell in the house of the Lord forever. Amen"* — Psalm 23, English Standard Bible

"Beloved, I wish above all things that thou mayest prosper and be in health, even as thy soul prospereth." — 3 John 2, King James Bible

" For I know the plans and thoughts that I have for you,' says the LORD, 'plans for peace and well-being and not for disaster, to give you a future and a hope. Then you will call on Me and you will come and pray to Me, and I will hear [your voice] and I will listen to you. Then [with a deep longing] you will seek Me and require Me [as a vital necessity] and [you will] find Me when you search for Me with all your heart." — Jeremiah 29:11-13, Amplified Bible

"Don't love money. Be happy with what you have because God has said, I will never abandon you or leave you." — Hebrews 13:5, God's Word Translation Bible

When someone says you cannot or should not continue living, tell them you are loved. Tell them you are wonderfully made. Tell them you are worthy and beautiful. Tell them that no one can steal your joy. Tell them you are a warrior, rich in understanding and strength.

You are beloved and let the love of Christ help you to take life as it comes but through his wisdom. Let the love in his words paint a beautiful landscape of hope to see his love better than what you are viewing now. Do not get caught up in the realities of others. The words of God teach all of us how to create a new and more truthful reality, for they are words infused with his love ensuring our success always.

Daughter always remember no matter the day, time or hour God is there for you. You are more precious than emeralds, pearls, diamonds or rubies. You are priceless and as his daughter, you are loved.

Reflection:

Write down ways you are special and how you see you are Loved by God

_____

_____

_____

_____

_____

_____

_____

_____

_____

_____

_____

_____

_____

_____

_____

_____

_____

_____

_____

_____

_____

Woman of Purpose

Every woman is strong and was made for a purpose in this world. I have listed women from the Bible later in this chapter who have used their lives to save others, themselves, lead others, and give birth to leaders for this world.

Let us give God the opportunity to have his Word be a "lamp unto your feet and light unto your path." Even the difficulties we experience, we can learn from; and they are designed where we can use them in the journey we are on. Let each of us identify with these women, who can be our examples of how important it is for us to live where we carry the spirit of "love, power and a sound mind." In God's eyes, we are not just daughters; we are princesses adorned with God's love, grace, and mercy. We can climb every mountain, cross every sea, and stand against the winds of adversity.

The Lord sees the mirror we look at and how it shows us a certain reflection. He also sees how the world is determined to give us another reflection of ourselves. It is up to us to not look to the left or right. God wants to cradle you in his arms and tell you do not let the integrity of who you are be compromised. The women I list never looked at the mirror image that society or culture reflected. They trusted in the reflective light of God's deliverance, protection, and wisdom.

Let these few examples of women from the Bible who trusted God in their adversity, serve as an encouragement for all of us.

Trustworthy

Ruth was trustworthy. She was willing to stay with her mother-in-law, Naomi. After the loss of Naomi's husband, she moved to an unfamiliar country and trusted in the God Naomi served. She was a friend and sincere daughter-in-law.

"Then Naomi said, 'Look, your sister-in-law has gone back to her people and to her gods; turn back and follow your sister-in-law.' But Ruth said, 'Do not urge me to leave

you or to turn back from following you; for where you go,
I will go, and where you lodge, I will lodge. Your people
will be my people, and your God, my God. Where you
die, I will die, and there I will be buried. May the Lord do
the same to me [as He has done to you], and more also, if
anything but death separates me from you. When Naomi
saw that Ruth was determined to go with her, she said
nothing more." — Ruth 1: 15-18. Amplified Bible

Faithful

The bent-over woman exemplifies the faithful servant. We do not know her name. but this woman went faithfully to the synagogue for many years, trusting God even though she was so far bent over that she could barely look directly at anyone. She blamed no one for her issue. She did not hate herself or others. She remained faithful and trusted God.

"And there was a woman who for eighteen years
had had an illness caused by a spirit (demon). She
was bent double and could not straighten up at all.
When Jesus saw her, He called her over and said to her,
'Woman, you are released from your illness'"
Then He laid His hands on her; and immediately
she stood erect again, and she began glorifying and
praising God." — Luke 13:11-15, Amplified Bible

Generous

The widow's offering exemplifies the generous giver. The widow gave from her heart, not her circumstance. She did not worry about what others thought. She was a generous giver because she trusted that God would meet her needs. Her financial circumstance did not define or stop who she was and her desire to live fully—trusting and believing.

> *"And He sat down opposite the [temple] treasury, and began watching how the people were putting money into the [a]treasury. And many rich people were putting in [b]large sums. A poor widow came and put in two small copper coins, which amount to a [c]mite. Calling His disciples to Him, He said to them, 'I assure you and most solemnly say to you, this poor widow put in [proportionally] more than all the contributors to the treasury. For they all contributed from their surplus, but she, from her poverty, put in all she had, all she had to live on" — Mark 12:41-44, Amplified Bible*

Courageous

The woman who washed Jesus' feet illustrates humility and courage. She was a woman known around town as being sinful, yet she sought out Jesus. She heard where he would be visiting and, on front of everyone, she bent down, washed his feet with her tears, and used her long flowing hair to gently dry his feet.

This woman was not afraid to show she was sorry for the life she was leading. She was courageous enough to let others see her remorse. The woman was grateful for the opportunity to change and thankful she could show just how much it meant to her. She was not afraid to show anyone how much God meant in her life.

"One of the Pharisees asked Jesus to eat with him, and He went into the Pharisee's house [in the region of Galilee] and reclined at the table. Now there was a woman in the city who was [known as] a sinner; and when she found out that He was reclining at the table in the Pharisee's house, she brought an alabaster vial of perfume; and standing behind Him at His feet, weeping, she began wetting His feet with her tears, and wiped them with the hair of her head, and [respectfully] kissed His feet [as an act signifying both affection and submission] and anointed them with the perfume." — Luke 7:36-38, Amplified Bible

Brave

Mary, mother of Jesus exemplifies courage and bravery. Mary was a woman willing to be used to bring the Savior into the world. Mary was brave, as she knew about the prophecy of Jesus, and was humbly ready to be obedient and strong enough to face what Jesus would go through in redeeming this world. She was a mother who loved and cared for her child and raised him, understanding his purpose for all humanity. She was brave every moment, knowing that Jesus belonged to the whole world. Mary had strength and taught us how to trust in God, knowing the plans he has for us—we are called to simply follow.

"For with God nothing [is or ever] shall be impossible."
Then Mary said, 'faith, Behold, I am the servant of the
Lord; may it be done to me according to your word.' And
the angel left her." — Luke 1:37-38, Amplified Bible

Prayer of Salvation

I pray the devotionals you have read touched your heart. The connection of the woman touching the hem of Jesus' garment, her healing, and Jesus comforting her, tells us how much God loves us. God, through his Son, wants to come into our lives to heal, restore, and make each of us whole in and through him.

Jesus came so that all can be free from sin. In the Word of God, Ephesians 3:20, we are told God is "able to do exceedingly abundantly above all we ask or think." God can do in our lives above our circumstances and how we think they are to be solved. Through our faith, God is able to do it.

He calls all of us to have faith and believe in him. Through him, it says in Romans 8:37, "We are more than conquerors." In Christ Jesus we are not conquered; we are conquerors. We are more than our problems, fears, and sorrows. We are more than what people say we are. We are undefeated and, through Christ, all things that seem impossible are possible.

God loves us so much that he sent his precious Son to redeem us from sin and save us. In John 3:16, God tells us he "so loved the world, that He gave His only begotten Son, that whoever believes in him and trusts in Him (as Savior) shall not perish, but have eternal life."

If today you desire Christ to come into your heart, please pray the Prayer of Salvation. In Romans 10:9, God tells us, "if we acknowledge and confess with our mouth that Jesus is Lord (recognizing His power, authority, and majesty as God) and believe in our heart that God raised Him from the dead, we will be saved."

"If we (freely) admit that we have sinned and confess
our sins, He is faithful and just (true to His own nature
and promises) and will forgive our sins and cleanse us
continually from all unrighteousness (our wrongdoing,
everything not in conformity with His will and purpose)."
— 1 John 1:9, Amplified Bible

"Dear Heavenly Father,

I believe the righteousness of God, as according to Romans 3:22, comes through faith in Jesus Christ. I believe, as according to Romans 6:23, that the wages of sin is death, but the free overwhelming gift of grace to believers is eternal life in Christ Jesus. Therefore, today I acknowledge and confess with my mouth that Jesus is Lord. I believe he died on the cross for my sins and was raised from the dead so that I would be saved. Jesus is the Son of God and I ask him now to come into my heart and I receive him as Lord of my life."

As according to 2 Corinthians 5:21, I believe with all my heart that I am now the righteousness of God and I thank God for coming into my heart. Amen!"

Date: _____

Signed: _____

Who We Are in Christ

This day you have prayed the prayer of Salvation and received Jesus Christ as your Lord and Savior. You are now a child of the most high God. The Lord laid on my heart to share with you some scriptures telling you who you are *now* in Christ. In this, you can start your relationship journey with Christ. He will never leave nor forsake you. He will walk with you every step of the way and the list that follows contains God's words letting you know he is for you.

Beautiful daughter, you are so loved and cherished. You are not alone. When all else fails, Christ will never, ever fail you. All you have to do is trust and believe—in this you will receive.

Please read and study the scriptures that follow, as the Lord says these words are for all of us:

"Let them not depart from thine eyes; keep them in the midst of thine heart." — Proverbs 4:21, King James Bible

Who We Are in Christ—Scriptures (Amplified Bible)

- I am now a new Creation in Christ

"Therefore, if anyone is in Christ [that is, grafted in, joined to Him by faith in Him as Savior], he is a new creature [reborn and renewed by the Holy Spirit]; the old things [the previous moral and spiritual condition] have passed away. Behold, new things have come [because spiritual awakening brings a new life]." — 2 Corinthians 5:17

- I am a child of God

"But to as many as did receive and welcome Him, He gave the right [the authority, the privilege] to become children of God, that is, to those who believe in (adhere to, trust in, and rely on) His name—" — John 1:12

- I am a friend of Jesus

"I do not call you servants any longer, for the servant does not know what his master is doing; but I have called you [My] friends, because I have revealed to you everything that I have heard from My Father." —John 15:15

- I am redeemed in Christ

"... and are being justified [declared free of the guilt of sin, made acceptable to God, and granted eternal life] as

a gift by His [precious, undeserved] [a]grace, through the redemption [the payment for our sin] which is [provided] in Christ Jesus," — Romans 3:24

- I am not condemned by Christ

  "Therefore, there is now no condemnation [no guilty verdict, no punishment] for those who are in Christ Jesus [who believe in Him as personal Lord and Savior]." — Romans 8:1

- I am accepted by Christ

  "Therefore, [continue to] accept and welcome one another, just as Christ has accepted and welcomed us to the glory of [our great] God." — Romans 15:7

- I am alive with Christ

  "Even when we were [spiritually] dead and separated from Him because of our sins, He made us [spiritually] alive together with Christ (for by His grace—His undeserved favor and mercy—you have been saved from God's judgment)." —Ephesians 2:5

- I am born of God; the evil one cannot touch me

  "We know [with confidence] that anyone born of God does not habitually sin; but He (Jesus) who was born of God [carefully] keeps and protects him, and the evil one does not touch him." — 1 John 5:18

- Greater is He that is in me
  "Little children (believers, dear ones), you are of God and you belong to Him and have [already] overcome them [the agents of the antichrist]; because He who is in you is greater than he (Satan) who is in the world [of sinful mankind]." — 1 John 4:4

- I have the peace of God
  "And the peace of God [that peace which reassures the heart, that peace] which transcends all understanding, [that peace which] stands guard over your hearts and your minds in Christ Jesus [is yours]." — Philippians 4:7

- I have the wisdom and revelation of God
  "[I always pray] that the God of our Lord Jesus Christ, the Father of glory, may grant you a spirit of wisdom and of revelation [that gives you a deep and personal and intimate insight] into the true knowledge of Him [for we know the Father through the Son]. And [I pray] that the eyes of your heart [the very center and core of your being] may be enlightened [flooded with light by the Holy Spirit], so that you will know and cherish the hope [the divine guarantee, the confident expectation] to which He has called you, the riches of His glorious inheritance in the saints (God's people)," — Ephesians 1:17-18

- I am free in Christ

  *"It was for this freedom that Christ set us free
  [completely liberating us]; therefore keep standing
  firm and do not be subject again to a yoke of slavery
  [which you once removed]." — Galatians 5:1*

- God can supply all my needs

  *"And my God will liberally supply (fill until full)
  your every need according to His riches in glory
  in Christ Jesus." — Philippians 4:19*

- I am chosen and royal

  *"But you are a chosen race, A royal priesthood,
  a consecrated nation, a [special] people for God's
  own possession, so that you may proclaim the
  excellencies [the wonderful deeds and virtues and
  perfections] of Him who called you out of darkness
  into His marvelous light." — 1 Peter 2:9*

- Christ lives in me

  *"I have been crucified with Christ [that is, in Him
  I have shared His crucifixion]; it is no longer I who live,
  but Christ lives in me. The life I now live in the body
  I live by faith [by adhering to, relying on, and completely
  trusting] in the Son of God, who loved me and gave
  Himself up for me." — Galatians 2:20*

Final Words

"A man's mind plans his way [as he journeys through life],
But the LORD directs his steps and establishes them."
— Proverbs 16:9, Amplified Bible

Dear Sisters in Christ,

Your journey now in Jesus Christ is not about perfection. There will be trials and tests. There will be times you are tempted but do not give up. Jesus is with you all, always. Study his Word and let his presence through his Word direct your thoughts, decisions and actions. When you are concerned, worried or afraid, trust God and, turn to his Word and prayer. If you do not already have a church home, I pray in my heart with you as you take your time to find a Bible-teaching church.

Please know God always meets us wherever we are in our lives. It is about how he builds us up, gives us strength, matures our hearts in him, and teaches us how to rely, adhere to, and live in his love and grace.

I wish this book could go on forever. I imagine us sitting together and sharing thoughts on God's amazing love, understanding, and the desires he has for our lives.

May the Lord bless and keep you. May he guide you, protect you and give you wisdom and revelation in the knowledge of Him. May God's mercy and grace be over your life this day and forevermore.

I leave you with the devotional below, which I composed when I first started writing.

"The words of the reckless pierce like swords...." — *Proverbs 12:18*

"The words of the mouth are deep waters..." — *Proverbs 18:4*

I'm Not That Word - The "B" Word
What was that word you just said? What makes you think this is who I am?

Words, words and more words; - there are so many spoken. There are words to remind us, embrace us, or destroy us. Words can be said to us to restrain or categorized us.

The one word that has become a mainstay in society is the "B" word. Everyone reading this knows exactly which word I am referring to. Each of us can unanimously agree we are not a female dog. Yet, today the dictionary has been revised to define it as a woman who is difficult or overbearing and a man who is weak.

We are not that word

We are not any word that calls someone outside their God-given name.

We are not that word that stamps us with a definition of hate or resentment.

We are not a word that intended to bring defamation to the woman we are.

We hear the "B" word in movies, read it in books, hear spoken on the street, sung in music, shouted in arguments, and whispered in workplaces.

We are not that word. Take a pen and paper and think of all the beauty you are. Make a list of the most positive words you know in the depth of your heart that you are. Take that list and go to the Word of God. Find scripture that supports the positive, life-giving words you wrote to describe yourself.

You are beautiful.

You are wonderful.

You are precious.

You are a rare gem.

You are the image of God.

You are magnificent.

You are worthy.

You are special.

You are a good thing.

You are loved.

As your sister in Christ, I tell you today, you are not what someone says, yesterday, today, or tomorrow, that contradicts the everlasting truth of what God says you are. Let these words hug you, kiss you, and hold you from my heart to yours.

You are all God says you are. Whenever someone tells you something different, go to God's word and find the scripture you searched for before and say it out loud and confess a different truth.

The world has words to say to imprison us, but God has words to free us. Stay in God's word and you will stay free—mentally, emotionally, and spiritually.

On the sixth day God had completed most of his creation, including humanity. This is what he saw:

"God saw all that he made, and it was very good...."
— *Genesis 1:31*

Are you a good thing to God....? Exactly!

Always remember that you are strong, beautiful, loved, and a good thing to God.

From my heart to yours,
Sherri

Coming Soon

in 2021!

Be sure to look out for the next devotional book called:

'I Choose to Walk in Faith Devotionals'

Excerpt from 'I Choose to Walk in Faith Devotionals'

Devotional: A Loving Faith

*"Peace be to the brethren, and love with faith,
from God the Father and the Lord Jesus Christ."*
— Ephesians 6:23 King James Bible

*"Remembering without ceasing your work of
faith, and labor of love, and patience of hope in our
Lord Jesus Christ, in the sight of God and our Father."*
— 1 Thessalonians 1:3 King James Bible

A Loving Faith

Faith is not just trusting God; it is also loving God. How do we live in a circle of loving faith? We do so by keeping a clear focus on God. We practice by using his words for they guide our actions and reactions to all things and people in our faith.

*God teaches us to have gentle peacefulness
in our response and actions.*

Faith is an attitude filled to the brim with gratitude. In other words, our gratefulness is overflowing. It flows in answers to those who hurt us, are angry toward us and cry out to us. Walking in faith is walking in perfect timing with the presence of God.

When we mumble and moan about our situations and surroundings, we pull ourselves away from the will of God's way of love. Complaining does not change things and in most cases makes them worse. Building our faith in the Lord teaches us to focus on the transformation needed within to radiate the beauty of Christ throughout our daily living.

Complaining evokes questioning. Mumbling reveals hints of doubt. Grumbling vibrates with negative impact to the surroundings we dwell in. Loving on the Lord, talking to the Lord, and listening to the spirit of the Lord is the most centered faith we can have. Faith is about tell us from the heart of God to stop, look and listen.

Stop trying to "figure it out", or do it in our own strength.

Look at where we are in our faith-based journey by the way we interact with others and handle our own circumstances.

Listen to the quietness of God's words of wisdom. Abide in his thoughts through his written Word. Remain faithful and still as he is already working things out. Negative attitudes produce negative outcomes. Positive attitudes produce love.

Life is a heartbeat of sights, sounds,
understandings and revelations.

Love in Christ is a dance with moves we are to follow to stay in step with him. Our faith lies where our
heart resides. Where will yours rest? Will it be in the
promises of God or in the words of the world?

A loving faith is trusting, believing, and
shaping our life around and through Christ.

Today, let us move in love. Let us answer others
with an understanding and caring word from scripture. Choose not to meet anger with anger or frustration with frustration. Think quickly but answer slow-
ly. Let the heart of Christ shine through reactions and
responses. God will smile as will others in our presence.

A loving faith in God is loving God because God is
love. His love is our love, so let us give love remembering that prayer and work change things and a loving
faith does too.

From my heart to yours,
Your sister in Christ,
Sherri

About the Author

Growing up in Long Island, New York, Sherri accepted Jesus Christ as her Lord and Savior at an early age. As an only child, Sherri enjoyed the creative arts, especially writing. Although she attended college, earning degrees in Hotel/Restaurant and Travel/Tourism, her heart always gravitated towards serving others. Since one of Sherri's favorite past times during college was writing poetry, after graduation she considered writing children storybooks – yet, God had another plan. When the Lord called Sherri to serve, Sherri waited on God to lead her. Years past and, after a great heartbreak, she began writing a small collection of devotionals filled with scripture intertwined with words of encouragement to herself. As time went on, these small writings grew and she began to share them with others. As Sherri's following grew, she decided to publish her first book. In this she finally understood what the Lord wanted her to do and Sherri has been writing ever since.

Sherri is active in her local church as a member of the Women's League ministry, donating her time to serve the Body of Christ as well as the local community. She hopes to bring a simple and clear understanding about the Lord to others and help lead many to Christ.

Made in United States
North Haven, CT
30 December 2021

13882841R00057